# Flower Arranging by Colour

A STEP-BY-STEP GUIDE TO
CREATING STUNNING DISPLAYS

DANA MARKOS AND SUSANNE CSONGOR

Packaged Goods
33 Commercial Street
Gloucester, MA 01930
(978) 282-9590

ISBN 1-84092-409-8

Printed in China.

10 9 8 7 6 5 4 3 2 1

Front and back cover images: Bobbie Bush Photography
Photography: Bobbie Bush Photography, bobbie@bobbiebush.com
Designer: Peter King & Company

Creative Direction: Silke Braun
Art and Photo Direction: Claire MacMaster
Editorial Director: Donna Raskin
Managing Editor: Brigid Carroll
Photo Editor: Jenny Beal

In memory of my maternal grandmother, Theodora, who showed me the path of beauty and love and my paternal grandmother, Vasiliki, who showed me perseverance and strength.
—DANA

In memory of my son, Mark.
—SUSANNE

# CONTENTS

# INTRODUCTION

## THE GLORIOUS WORLD OF COLOR AND FLOWERS

Flowers appeal to so many of our senses at once—their color and design touch our sight, their scent infuses our brain with pleasant sensations, while their texture gives pleasure to both our eyes and hands. Floral arrangements take those sensations one step further because floral design uses color, scent, and texture to create an unexpected surprise of beauty and intensity. Over the years, these arrangements have changed as much as other elements of design, such as fashion and home decor. The carnation corsage of the 1940s and 1950s seems dated to us today, while the huge, fussy flower arrangements of the 1980s seem overblown and loud compared to the simplicity of today's floral designs.

And it's not just design that dictates change in floral arrangements. For instance, the meanings of bridal bouquets have changed throughout history. In medieval times, women carried aromatic bunches of herbs and garlic to ward off bad spirits. Hawaiian brides and grooms have worn leis and Native Americans favor floral headdresses.

Victorian women were among the first to tie small bunches of flowers together with lace and ribbons. These nosegays were created with different flowers in a variety of colors, but today we see one-color themes, such as the all-white bouquet. The twenty-first-century bride might even choose to simply group one type of flower, such as calla lilies, for a dramatic effect.

Choosing and combining flowers takes a clever mind, a sensitive eye, and a patient hand. The designer of any arrangement strives to send a flower-filled message of love or passion, the beauty of elegance, or the excitement of nature and wilderness.

Each design in this book features a combination of colors and textures designed to accentuate the room and vase they are placed in, as well as to complement the host or the bride who is holding them. As a florist and poet once wrote:

*"The varied colours run: and while they break*
*On the charmed eye, the exulting florist marks,*
*With secret pride, the wonders of his hand."*

# The Story of a Secret Garden

Our studio, A Secret Garden, is set in the beautiful North Shore of Boston with a very serene view of the Ipswich Reservoir. This natural backdrop is a source of inspiration and spirituality for our art. We watch the seasons change along the banks and find solace and comfort in nature's wonders. This muse allows us to communicate to others through the designs we create for them.

But we weren't always so fortunate. We both came to floral design after spending part of our lives working hard in other fields.

## DANA'S STORY

Like so many people in their midthirties, I admitted something life-changing to myself one day—I had a job for which I had no passion. In fact, although I worked hard for seventeen years as a banker and corporate trainer, it was only a job and it simply didn't feed my soul.

A friend once pointed out that I had been given a talent to bring beauty into the lives of others through my floral arrangements. And from that day forward, I chose to live my passion—to feel it and never take it for granted or treat it casually.

It was scary to start a new business and a new life, but I knew I had a few things going for myself. I had a tremendous work ethic, a lot of determination, and most importantly, I had the incredible love and support of my wife, children, and friends.

## SUSANNE'S STORY

My career was born from necessity. A young mother with four small children, I simply needed a job during a downturn in my life. I loved flowers, so I got a job cleaning a floral shop for one year. That was how long it took before I was even allowed to touch the flowers. I kept my mouth shut and my hands busy and I ended up learning an awful lot from my boss before it was time to move on.

After taking a new job at a different floral shop, I attended a floral design program, where I was eventually asked to join the faculty. Instead I took a job designing silk floral arrangements, believing that it was more important to keep learning than to teach what I already knew.

Then, in what we consider to be a moment that was meant to be, Dana and I met at a wedding facility where we were both arranging flowers. We clicked right then and there, and have been together ever since.

Patience, respect, interpretation, and artistry—these are all important to being a designer and working with flowers. In many of our lectures we often speak about listening to each flower, because we believe that each one has a voice. People may laugh, but we believe that if you take the time to feel each flower in your hand, it will help guide you in your arranging.

We have designed for *Art in Bloom* and WGBH (Boston Public Television). We lecture for numerous garden clubs, and, of course, we have provided the floral designs and arrangements for hundreds (and now, almost thousands) of weddings and events.

But our accomplishments are not nearly as meaningful to us as the role we have played in people's lives. We travel with people through their most joyous occasions and their saddest reflections. We would like to share a story about one bride, Sammie. She was suffering from cancer while she planned her wedding in May of 1998. We breathed every joyful breath with her on that day. Then, with our hearts heavy, we mourned with her family in late 1999 when we were honored to provide them with flowers at the time of her passing.

We believe that Sammie is an example of someone who, despite everything, lived passionately. And so, with her spirit as our guide, and our own story as an example, we would like to encourage each of you to find your passion and live it. It is never too late and each one of you is here to make a difference, and to pass on a message through your passion.

This book represents some of our passion. Thank you for joining us on this journey.

Many blessings,
Dana & Susanne

# CHAPTER 1

## Color Choices

### THINKING ABOUT THE SETTING

Flowers, whether set in an arrangement or a bouquet, are part of an overall scene. They are either an accessory that contributes to the background look of a room or event, or they are an ornament that helps to change a room from one type of place to another.

Consider, for example, a high-tech urban loft with black leather furniture and exposed pipes hanging from the ceiling. Now fill that room with buckets of daisies. The flowers immediately change the atmosphere, and you might wonder if there is romance in the air. Take away those buckets of daisies and add a few single orchids in clear glass cylinders around the room and, once again, the room has changed.

The first step in designing a flower arrangement is to consider the style of the room in which it will be placed. How would you describe the furniture? What other accessories are placed on the shelves or mantels? Is the space brightly lit or dark? Is the lighting natural and coming through open windows, or do fluorescent bulbs light the space?

The answers to these questions will help you decide which flowers to choose for your arrangement, and they will also guide you toward the "look" you want to achieve with your design.

We've created a chart to give you some flower suggestions that might work with the different types of rooms and events you will encounter.

You'll also want to ask yourself how you want to use your arrangements and how many you want to make. Will your flowers be used simply as a welcoming element in a home, or will you be decorating tables for a large party? Do you want people to see through the arrangement to the wall, so that their eyes get a "break" from clusters of flowers, or do you want the flowers to look overflowing and abundant in their container? An open arrangement is soothing and peaceful, while a full arrangement looks lush and rich.

You've probably noticed that we didn't suggest that you begin your arrangement preparations by seeing what flowers are available. These days, it's possible to get almost any kind of flower you want, at almost all times of the year. So, you are free to let your imagination run wild when coming up with a design.

# Color Chart

| | | BLUES/PURPLES | YELLOWS |
|---|---|---|---|
| DÉCOR | Industrial | Moth Orchid | Amaryllis |
| | Country | Scabiosa | Iris 'Apollo' <br> Swamp Rose Mallow |
| | Contemporary | Iris <br> Harebell | Narcissi <br> 'Yellow Cheerfulness' |
| | Italian | Campanula | Craspedia |
| | Neoclassic | Hydrangea | Daffodil |
| LIGHTING | Sunny | Grape Hyacinth <br> Forget-Me-Not | Sunflower |
| | Dark | Light Blue Iris <br> Greater Fringed Gentian | Rose 'Hollywood' |
| | Well-Lit by Bulbs | Anemone | Icelandic Poppy |
| | Candlelight | Anemone <br> 'Mona Lisa Blue' <br> Late Purple Aster | Yellow Calla Lily |
| EVENT | Wedding | Hydrangea <br> 'Sarah Bernhardt' | Tulip |
| | Luncheon | Cymbidium Orchid <br> Showy Aster | Rose 'Ambience' |
| | Bridal Shower | Pansy | Daffodil <br> Buttonweed |
| | Informal Dinner | Allium | Sunflowers <br> Cuckoo Flower |
| | Formal Dinner | Anemone | French Tulip |
| | Outdoor Party | Phlox <br> Morning Glory | Marigold |

| WHITES | REDS/PINKS | GREENS | ORANGES | |
|---|---|---|---|---|
| Madonna Lily<br>Ming Fern<br>Typha | Clematis | Bear Grass | Birds of Paradise | |
| Daisy | Ranunculus | Limonium<br>Ivy | Ranunculus | |
| | Gloriosa<br>Rothschildiana | Apidstra<br>Bamboo | Parrot Tulips | |
| Casablanca Lily<br>Greendragon | Gerbera | Galax | Zinnia | |
| Water Lily | Tulips<br>Pale Green Orchid | Viburnum | Rose | |
| Trillium<br>Wood Anemone | Anthurium | Lemon Leaf | Tulips | |
| Canada Violet | Red Poppy | Seeded Eucalyptus | Gerbera 'Clementine' | |
| Tulips | Spray Carnation | Ivy | Carnation | |
| Lisianthus | Rose 'Souvenir' | Bamboo | Rose 'Orange Unique' | |
| Peony<br>Eucalyptus | Rose 'Charlotte' | Seeded Eucalyptus | Mango Calla Lily | |
| Asiatic Lily<br>Pittosporum | Rose 'Candy Bianca' | Italian Variegated<br>Pittosporum | Yellow-Fringed Orchid | |
| Lily of the Valley | Primrose | Rose 'Leonides' | Painted Cup | |
| White Viburnum | Spirea<br>Leafy Splurge | Eucalyptus | Orange Hawkweed | |
| Rose 'Nicole' | Anthurium | Ivy | Sunflower | |
| Sweet Pea | Stock | Love Lies Bleeding<br>Rosemary | Birds of Paradise | |

# Complements and Contrasts

Everyone knows there are three primary colors (red, blue, yellow) and two other basic colors: black and white. Combine those hues and you can come up with any number of colors.

The secondary colors, which are created by blending two of the primary colors, are orange, green, and violet. Combine a primary color with an adjacent secondary color and you've got the six tertiary colors: red-orange, red-violet, yellow-green, yellow-orange, blue-green, and blue-violet.

Designers and artists use specific terms to describe the ways in which colors work together.

**Complementary colors** sit directly opposite each other on the color wheel. **Analogous colors** are three consecutive hues of the color wheel. **Monochromatic colors** are one primary color and any or all of its tints and shades. **Split complementary colors** are one hue and the two hues on either side of its complement. For example: red, yellow-green, and blue-green.

**Clashing colors** sit next to each other on the color wheel.

## DETERMINING YOUR COLOR PALETTE

In flower arranging, you're not combining colors to create new colors. Instead, you're putting colors next to each other to create a mood or a feeling. For example, if you put a deep red rose next to a white rose, you're using color to send a message. We associate red with passion and white with innocence.

Some color associations are emotional and somewhat colloquial (we all know that red roses mean love), but for a floral designer it's important to understand the aesthetics of colors, too. Red is not only our culture's sign of love, but also the complement to green, according to the color wheel.

A color palette simply describes the colors you want to use for each arrangement. For example, you could decide that for a baby shower, you want to use a pastel color scheme featuring purple, pink, and green. That would be your color palette. With those colors in mind, when you go to the florist, you might opt to use pale roses, lilacs, and some ferns to create your arrangement.

A TINT OF A COLOR IS MADE BY ADDING WHITE TO A PRIMARY COLOR. A SHADE IS MADE BY ADDING BLACK

Some color palette options are:

**Monochromatic:** One hue in combination with any or all of its tints and shades. Pink and red roses, for instance. Even if you choose a monochromatic palette, it's important to remember that no two colors of anything are "exactly" the same; therefore, the slight shading differences will help to create subtle texture in an arrangement or bouquet.

**Vibrant:** Bright, true tones of the primary and secondary colors. This color palette could easily look too flamboyant, as its vividness would actually take away from the beauty of each bloom. However, one or two vibrant colors often look beautiful next to complementary shades and against a background of greens.

**Pastel:** Pale colors that have a lot of white. Pink roses, yellow daffodils, and lilacs are good examples of pastel-hued flowers. These blossoms are gentle to the eye, and, because they blend well with other pastel flowers, you can mix numerous shades together in an arrangement or bouquet.

**Jewel:** Deep, vivid colors that combine vibrant tones with black. Who isn't struck by the regal appearance of a crimson rose or a deep purple anemone? These shades produce quite an impact on the eye, and rarely will you need to use an abundance of them to make a statement. Instead, jewel-toned flowers can be used sparingly, but to great effect.

If you choose a varied color palette, remember to shade the flowers up and down within the color wheel of that palette. By doing so, you'll allow the different colors to play off each other, which will illuminate the different textures of your flowers.

## THE LANGUAGE OF COLOR

As we mentioned above, in our culture, we have come to identify red roses with love and passion, but what do other colors mean? Here are some ideas to help you determine which colors you want to include in your arrangements:

Besides being associated with love, **red** also looks regal and aristocratic.

**Yellow** is a happy, friendly color. Too much yellow can be overwhelming, but it often looks nice against white, green, and blue.

Hues from **red** to **yellow**, including **orange**, **pink**, **brown**, and **burgundy**, are considered warm. Warm colors are cheerful and energetic.

**Green** is always associated with nature, and therefore often makes us feel tranquil. Bright green looks more youthful than dark green, which can be almost poetic. Cool colors, such as green and violet, are calming.

The color of the sky and the sea, **blue** is a calm, peaceful, cool color. Royal and navy blue are much more conservative colors than sky blue.

One of the few places **purple** doesn't look funky is on a flower. However, too much purple can often look gaudy, while a well-placed deep purple has a regal effect.

**White** can be elegant or innocent, depending on which flower it graces (lilies or daisies, for example). It's also important to remember that white flowers are often highly scented.

In general, **light** colors are poetic and easily draw attention from the eye, but they shouldn't be confused with "dull" colors, that is, pastels that aren't bright.

**Dark**, **deep** colors, such as burgundy and purple, are good accent colors, but often give an arrangement a heavy feel. Vivid colors, such as bright red, yellow, or orange, are emotional.

# CHAPTER 2

## CHOOSING FLOWERS

Of course, color is not the only thing that matters when creating a flower arrangement. There are a few shapes to consider: domed, spiky, single bloom, floating, grouped, and open. Texture is also important. Some flowers have full heads, while others have petals that are easily visible. Contrasting these types of textures can add visual interest. Foliage also adds a bit of variation, so while most bouquets arrive with ferns, consider adding eucalyptus (which has a wonderful scent), grasses, and other greens to stimulate the eye and flatter the flowers within your arrangement.

**Flowers are divided into three shapes:**

**Round,** such as roses and carnations.

**Vertical,** such as gladioli and delphiniums. Vertical flowers are regal, and can be accented with shorter leaves to the front and sides of the arrangement.

**Transitional,** such as cornflowers or lisianthus (they look like stepping-stones).

Don't be afraid of stems and foliage. Consider them another element of the flower that is part of the design.

Also, don't forget to consider the size of each bloom. Larger flowers easily overshadow smaller ones, so in order to make sure little blossoms stand out, you usually need to be in contrasting shades. If you're sticking to a monochromatic palette, you might want to cluster a bunch of smaller blooms together so that they create a comparable impact in size.

When choosing flowers, consider, too, how much care you will be able to give them while they are in the arrangement. Delicate flowers that need to be in water for a long time, such as lily of the valley, may not last through an entire event, especially if the weather is very hot. Likewise, if you're going to decorate for a nighttime affair in the morning, choose flowers that will stand the wait, and make sure that someone will be around to water and perk up the arrangement later in the day.

## ORDERING FLOWERS

⚘ Flowers look beautiful outside, but buy ones that have been stored inside, preferably inside a refrigerator, as that keeps them healthier. Tight buds need a few days to open fully and flowers that are already fully open have passed their peak.

⚘ Establish the essence of the design in your mind, and choose greens that will complement your arrangement. There are many greens available to accent the arrangement, from dark green to a sage color, to variegated combinations. In addition to the shading of greens, their different textures also add an interesting factor to any arrangement. The color and texture of the flowers will help you determine which greens are better to use for your particular arrangement.

⚘ Create a flower order, as well as a list of supplies that you will need. It is helpful to sit down and think about how many stems of each flower you will need to complete your project. Make a list of each type of flower and include the greens you will need as well. Don't forget all the additional supplies, such as knives (never scissors), wire, tape, and also include the container and the insert you need to protect the container.

⚘ Are you using your own flowers, rather than ordering them? Be sure to cut them from the garden early in the morning, never in the middle of the day when it's hottest. Place the blooms in water immediately. Using clippers or a knife, make a diagonal cut, which leaves more of the cells open for absorbing water.

## CARING FOR FLOWERS

⚘ Flower arrangements, whether in a vase, a basket, or a bouquet, have to be handled like artwork. Just as a painter has to learn how to stretch canvas and care for brushes, floral designers have to understand their "tools," in order to keep plants and flowers healthy and vibrant. Flowers are alive and we must treat them in a way that supports good health.

⚘ Make sure any vase, basket, or other piece of sculpture that is going to hold your arrangement is clean. This is especially important if you're reusing a vase or basket, since bacteria from previous arrangements can contaminate new stems. Plastic storage containers are better for plants than metal ones, so if you're using a copper bucket, for example, to hold flowers, insert a plastic container inside the bucket, to keep the flowers healthy.

⚘ It's important to use preservatives, which are available at most floral shops, to keep flowers lasting a long time. Since chemicals and hard minerals can block the flow of water in the stems of flowers, try to use the purest water you're able to get. Make sure the water sits for half an hour before putting flowers into it, so it reaches room temperature and all of the air has escaped.

⚘ Add the flowers to the water in the storage bucket, allowing them to hydrate for another half-hour before placing them in the arrangement, so they don't dry out. Just let them stand loosely, and make sure they aren't in bright sun, which will wilt them.

figure 1

figure 2

 Once it's time to begin your creation, remove the lower leaves of each stem (figure 1). Always use sharp cutting tools, because ragged edges can prevent water from properly nourishing the stems.

 Although florists keep flowers in "refrigerators," they really aren't at refrigerator temperature. They have special humidity levels and fans; do not put your flowers in your refrigerator at home for longer than a half-hour to an hour.

 If, during the course of an event, an individual flower dies within an arrangement, remove it. Sometimes, if a flower looks a little tired, it helps to trim the stem and remove some of the foliage. Put the flower in warm water for a bit, as this might help it perk up.

 Water tubes may also be hidden within arrangements to ensure continued hydration of the stems (figure 2). Simply fill the tube with water, replace the cap, and insert the stem into the hole. Water tubes are especially helpful in arrangements in which a container cannot be used, such as a banister decoration for the holidays.

 Certain flowers require more detailed care. For example, semi-woody stemmed flowers, such as some poppy varieties, are considered "milky" because they have a sap. This sap can kill the other flowers in an arrangement. You need to cauterize the stems to seal in the sap. Plunge them into boiling water for ten seconds, or put them over a candle flame until the ends are sealed. The stem itself will have enough water to keep the plant alive. Solid woody stems, such as peonies and hydrangeas, do not need to be cauterized.

 Be sure to trim any leaves that will be below the water line, especially if you're using a clear glass vase. Crush the ends of thick stems to help them absorb water. Change a vase's water every other day. Add new clean water to a vase and let the excess overflow until the water runs clear.

 Every rose has what is called guard petals and they do just that, guard the inside petals of the rose. Whenever you are using roses, remove all guard petals from each rose. Guard petals sit on the outside of the bloom; they look less mature than the rest of the flower and are often slightly less than perfect.

# CHAPTER 3

# The Architecture of Flower Arranging

As with all of the great art forms, much of what makes flower arranging so spectacular is invisible to the eye of the viewer. Just as a person watching a ballerina can't imagine how many hours she practiced each step, or how difficult it is to hold her arm just so, most people don't understand that it's not just the flowers that make an arrangement beautiful. A floral designer knows how to cut, treat, and support an arrangement, then decorate it with bows or other ornaments to make it long lasting and healthy, as well as pleasing to the eye.

Now we will show you how to stabilize a container. This is core to the world of designing. Good, strong techniques will inevitably support any arrangement, but more importantly, the skill you develop through this process will come in very handy someday—and on many occasions when it is least expected.

Remember, anything can be a "vase." Objects that flatter flowers include buckets, wood boxes, baskets, and jars. If someone sends you (or hands you) a bouquet of flowers, don't automatically reach for the leftover vase you have. Think about which type of container would best suit these flowers. Daisies, for example, which are sweet and informal, look wonderful in a fruit jar or piled loosely in a basket. A single tulip can look elegant in a ceramic sculpture. As a general rule, flowers should be twice the height of a container, but don't get too concerned about that detail; your eye is a better judge of how well a container suits a bouquet.

If you want to use a vase, don't head straight for translucent crystal. Look for vases in a variety of colors (blue or green glass is often a good choice), as well as in a variety of materials.

To turn any type of container into a vase, just make sure it is very clean and watertight. If it's not, insert a plastic flower holder. If a container is slightly weathered, tie a ribbon around it or wrap it in cloth to give it a fresh look.

We are going to prepare three containers: a basket, an urn, and a vase. Each container needs to be handled in a specific way in order for it to hold flowers properly, but they have one thing in common—each container needs an oasis.

An oasis is a synthetic block that soaks up water and can hold flower stems securely. When the oasis is submerged in water with the pinholes facing up, it releases air bubbles as it becomes wet.

Once you remove the oasis from the water, you can cut it to fit the container you have chosen. Most of the time, you will have to secure the oasis using ¼-inch floral tape. This adds stability, especially during the transport of the arrangement.

1.

2.

3.

4.

## HOW TO PREPARE A BASKET

1. People love to buy baskets, but they often keep them around the house empty, which is a real shame. Baskets are a natural container for flowers. The only things you'll need to create flower-friendly baskets are plastic liners, a variety of oases, scissors, and floral tape to keep the oasis in place.

2. Add the liner to protect your basket and to hold water to feed your arrangements. Many people mistakenly believe that a steady supply of water is all that a flower arrangement needs once it's been created, but our next step, creating the oasis, will make the difference between a sturdy arrangement and a collection of loose flowers. Be sure to soak your oasis before placing it in the liner.

3. Insert the oasis into the liner (sometimes you have to tape it in to keep it secured). An oasis works best when it fits snugly into the container, so you may have to stuff smaller pieces around the larger piece in the center. The more oasis you use, the more mass you have available for your flower stems, which means a lusher arrangement.

4. Tape in the oasis by taking a strip of ¼-inch green floral tape and wrapping one end around the base of the handle (where the handle meets the rim) and stretching it across to the other side of the basket. Attach it to that handle. Turn the basket halfway around and attach another strip of tape across the basket to make a cross.

## HOW TO PREPARE AN URN

1. These steps will work for any container that isn't necessarily a vase. These instructions, like these types of containers, are perfect for long-stemmed flowers or a large number of short-stemmed flowers. You will need a large, clear piece of plastic (or a clear plastic garbage bag), oasis, floral tape, and scissors.

2. Line the urn with an abundant amount of plastic to protect it from water. Push it down as far as possible into the urn. If it slides around, you can use floral tape to keep it secure, but only use a little bit at the bottom, as you'll want to be able to maneuver the plastic a bit after you add the oasis and flowers.

3. Add the soaked oasis, making sure it fits securely and won't slide against the plastic. Once again, use tape, if necessary, to keep the oasis steady. As you can see, we add a lot of oasis to all of our containers. Smaller pieces may fit into the container more neatly, but it will make the flower arranging a bit more awkward. Remember the mass of flowers will hide the oasis (as well as the plastic).

4. Trim the plastic so it isn't visible. However, don't cut the plastic below the rim of the urn, as you may find you need to move the oasis around as you add flowers. Remember, too, that the plastic serves to protect the urn, so you can always use greens to hide plastic.

1.

2.

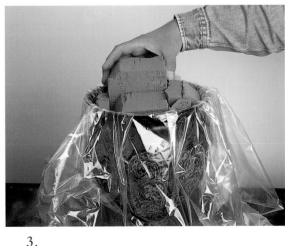

3.

4.

## HOW TO PREPARE A VASE

1. You won't always have an oasis on hand, especially if you're fortunate enough to receive a delivery of flowers. There is an easy way, however, to create a beautiful arrangement simply by using tape—even regular clear tape.

   Take two strips of clear ¼-inch tape and place them across the top of the vase, securing the ends to the rim. Turn the vase and place three going in the opposite direction of the other two, creating a grid.

2. Run a piece of tape around the rim to further secure the edges of the grid.

3. Choose greens that will complement the container and the arrangement.

4. Adding greens to your container is considered "setting the bones" for the rest of the arrangement. By doing this you establish the beginning of the arrangement and the lines you will follow when you begin adding flowers.

5. Arrange your flowers in proportion to the container and to each other. Larger flowers, or "line" flowers as they are often called, further establish the lines of the arrangement. However, it is also important to play on their size by adding others that are smaller in size and have less "weight" of color.

6. Finally, when you are arranging, not all the flowers need to be on the same plane. Create depth by lowering and weaving the heights of the stems you insert. Your arrangement should look as if it is a growing piece. Remember, flowers do not grow in any garden at the same height and size, so do not design them like that, or you will end up with an arrangement that doesn't flow and seems too contrived.

7. Shorter flowers toward the front add depth to an arrangement, and grouping flowers together adds impact. Often people will simply "mix up" all of their blooms, but this can actually take away from the viewers' ability to "see" each flower.

8. When your arrangement is done, remove all scraps and other items that may be interfering with your view and ability to give it perspective. Step away and look at the arrangement with "fresh" eyes. Try to see it as a stranger might and make any adjustments you feel are necessary.

9. And remember, beauty is in the eye of the beholder, and though there may be right or wrong ways to do some things in design, you have just created a very personal reflection of your talents and yourself. Enjoy it.

TOOLS, LEFT TO RIGHT: *gauge wire; chenille; tapes: ¼-inch green waterproof tape, double-sided tape, ¼-inch clear waterproof tape, green floral tape; cowie pick; knife; needle nose pliers; clippers; scissors*

## TOOLS

It takes a lot of effort to get flowers to stand up straight, or to keep three different types of flowers bound together. And, of course, all of this work has to be invisible to the eye. Here's what you'll need to create these arrangements. These items are available at most craft shops as well as floral supply stores. Ask your local florist where they gets theirs, or feel free to use the resources at the back of this book.

**Waterproof tape:** It comes in white, green, and clear. Get all three. This sticks to pottery, metal, plastic, wood, and, of course, stems.

**Waterproof clay:** Use this like glue, to position candles and figures in an arrangement, or to hold fruit in cornucopia displays. It must be completely dry and dust-free to stick.

**Glue gun:** You'll need this to adhere ribbons and other accessories to an arrangement.

**Floral stem tape:** It stretches and sticks to itself so you can make stems the same length.

**Anchor pins:** These secure stems to the oasis.

**Floral wires or stem wires:** These come in different sizes and gauges; the higher the gauge number, the more flexible and thinner the wire. They can be spooled or cut. These wires allow you to support a stem or to attach stems to one another.

**Candle cups:** You can use these to place candles in arrangements. Stick some tape under the cup to place it in an arrangement.

**Foam:** There are many types of floral foams. Foam allows flowers to stay in place and to get water at the same time. This is the same thing as an oasis. Nonporous foams, such as plastic, Styrofoam, or desert foam, are good for silk and dried arrangements.

# Ribbons

There is an art to ribbons—choosing the right ones, tying them well, and knowing when too much is too much and when just a little is all you need.

Many of today's beautiful ribbons owe their magnificence to technology. Ribbons of all kinds of textures can hold their shape because flexible wires are woven into the fabric. And many of today's ribbons are two-sided, so you don't have to worry about tying your bow and ending up with the "wrong" side facing out.

In general, **velvet** ribbons are good for holidays and for arrangements that are done in the winter. They have a formal appeal.

**Satin** ribbons can have cut or woven edges. They are very fluid. Some have wire in them to hold their shape.

**Taffeta** ribbons are lively, with prints on them.

**Moiré** ribbon shimmers and looks best on centerpieces rather than bouquets, as it can overwhelm them. It is good for large bows.

**Grosgrain** ribbon and **faille** are heavier than taffeta. They make "lazy" bows, which can look fun and informal.

**Piqué-edged** bows are very youthful and work well with arrangements that will be used by small children, such as flower girls and ring bearers.

**French wire** ribbons have many colors and textures, but the important thing to know is that they hold their shape well and allow you to use the ribbon for dramatic effect. Metallic mesh is good for wreaths.

**Organdy** and **chiffon** are soft and fluffy, often transparent. These work well for wedding and baby showers and more feminine events.

**Brocade** is usually used for trims with velvet. Of course, you can use lots of other materials to accessorize your bouquets and arrangements, such as burlap, lace, and tulle.

## Beautiful Bows

Bows are as important to flower arranging as the greens that surround the blooms. The bow is usually round.

*On the left, a two-loop bow and, on the right, a round multiloop.*

1. *Holding the ribbon in both hands, pinch the ribbon and form a loop.*

2. *Twist the ribbon and form another loop. Continue on, keeping one hand secure around the base of the loops.*

3. *Use wire to secure knots in your floral bows.*

4. *Cut the ends of ribbons on the diagonal, or make two cuts from each end of the ribbon in an inverted "V."*

## HOW TO MAKE FLORAL BOWS

A floral bow has two or more loops. If there are more than two, the larger ones are on the outside and the smaller ones are in the center.

1. Pinch the ribbon and make a loop, leaving the tail at the length you want.

2. Make a full twist of the ribbon and make another loop, with the right side of the ribbon facing out. Continue making loops, gradually increasing their size until the bow is full and you have enough ribbon to make another tail. The loops line up one on top of the other. Adjust the tails so that each has the right side facing out.

3. Secure the center of the bow with wire. Cut the tails of the bows in angles or points.

4. Fan out the loops and cut the ends of the ribbon diagonally.

# CHAPTER 4

*Dinner Centerpieces*

# Magical Candlelight

This centerpiece will look perfect in either a casual afternoon tea setting or a more formal dinner party. It's romantic and lush, and at the same time, colorful and muted, with its combination of white, pink, and lavender flowers against the background of various greens. We placed a small votive candle in the middle of the arrangement to create a more intimate atmosphere.

### FLOWERS

5 tulips
7 lisianthus
5 anemones
10 grape hyacinths
5 scabiosas
7 'Candy Bianca' roses
7 blue delphiniums

### MATERIALS

5 lamb's ears
10 stems leather leaf
3 stems Italian variegated
  pittosporum
4 caspias
clippers
floral tape
votive
oasis

1.

2.

## DESIGN

1. Soak the oasis in water until fully saturated (about ten to fifteen minutes). Then use floral tape to secure the oasis in the bowl, including clear tape across the top and onto the sides. Clean the flowers of any old or unattractive leaves, but don't clean them entirely; their leaves will add color to the arrangement.

2. Create a nice base of green, particularly focusing on using the lamb's ear, leather leaf, and pittosporum. Using the green first helps you establish a good visual background for the flowers. Vary the greens without overfilling.

3.

4.

3. Begin by inserting the lavender flowers. Turn the arrangement as you add flowers. When you see enough of the dominant color, start adding other colors to augment and accentuate the originals. Layer the colors to your personal taste. There shouldn't be a front or back to the arrangement. Interact with the arrangement and respond to the flowers as you place them.

4. Begin adding the smaller flowers, including the hyacinth, caspia, and lamb's ears. The final touch in this arrangement is the dried scabiosa buds that add interest to the otherwise lush bouquet.

## color options

FOR AN ARRANGEMENT THAT features pink and white, we suggest (top to bottom):

1. pink ranunculus

2. deep pink rose

3. pink chinamum

4. hibiscus

# Tuscan Abundance

Everyone loves the feeling of Tuscany. Entertain your guests with a combination of fruits and flowers to create feelings of old-world warmth, comfort, and abundance, from the lush rose to the meaty color of the beautiful calla lily. Include lady's apples and small pears to complete the arrangement for a Sunday dinner of close family and friends.

**3.**

**2.**

**4.**

## DESIGN

1. Soak the oasis in water for approximately ten to fifteen minutes. Then secure it to the container using ¼-inch green waterproof tape. Clean flowers of loose foliage, but leave healthy-looking leaves to create good texture within the arrangement.

2. Begin inserting larger flowers first, to create a line that will determine the size of your arrangement.

3. Fill in with the smaller flowers, alternating the types you place. This method will allow you to let each color and shape play off the other individual flowers.

4. Using greens, berries, fruits, and mosses, fill in the arrangement, creating a design that is thick and rich. Check the final arrangement from all vantage points so that you can be sure none of the materials used are showing.

FLOWERS CAN ADD A PERFECT TOUCH TO A THEMED DINNER PARTY. MANY CUISINES CAN BE EASILY PAIRED WITH SPECIFIC BLOOMS AND TYPES OF ARRANGEMENTS. FOR EXAMPLE, JAPANESE FLORAL DECORATION TENDS TO BE SIMPLE AND OPEN; FRENCH ARRANGEMENTS ARE EITHER LUSH AND INFORMAL FOR THE COUNTRY, OR ELEGANT AND STREAMLINED FOR A MORE PARISIAN LOOK.

Dazzle your guests with this spectacular show of nature's breathtaking creation: the calla lily! This is one of our favorite designs because it is so simple and yet truly elegant.

## FLOWERS

*8 calla lilies*
*3 icicle branches*

## MATERIALS

*clippers*
*round mirror*
*tall vase*
*silver glitter*

## DESIGN

1. Fill a glass cylinder with water, not quite to the top. You will not need to trim the branches too much, as they should rise tall from the cylinder after you insert them.

2. Cut the calla lilies with a knife to get a clean edge. Then insert them, allowing their stems to touch the edge of the vase, which will hold them up.

3. Place the completed arrangement on a round mirror, about 11–12 inches in diameter. Sprinkle the arrangement with silver glitter and make any final adjustments to the flowers, just in case they moved when you carried the arrangement to where it will sit.

Ce ORDER CALLA LILIES WITH LONG STEMS TO ENSURE THAT THEY WILL BE IN PROPORTION TO THE CYLINDER YOU HAVE CHOSEN TO ARRANGE THEM IN. NOTE: WHEN THE WATER IN A VASE IS VISIBLE IN AN ARRANGEMENT, YOU CAN ADD A DROP OF BLEACH TO KEEP THE WATER CLEAR.

1.

2.

3.

# Spring Uprising

This arrangement will encourage your guests' minds to wander. They will fantasize about the sun getting warmer day by day and envision all of the bulbs they planted in late fall straining to burst in all their glory. We created vignettes within the arrangement to suggest the image of a springtime walk.

### FLOWERS

| | |
|---|---|
| 5 pink bouvardias | 5 freesias |
| 5 blue or purple irises | 7 yellow daffodils |
| 3 viburnums | 1 stem split genestra |
| 3 spray roses | 7 pink and purple hyacinths |
| 3 stocks | 3 blue or purple anemones |
| 5 chartreuse roses | 1 stem split wax flower |
| 3 purple statices | 3–5 delphiniums |
| 5 sweet pea vines | |

### MATERIALS

| | |
|---|---|
| 3 curly willow branches | scissors |
| green ivy | floral knife |
| shittake mushrooms | clippers |
| bulbs | ¼-inch waterproof tape |
| sheet moss | plastic sheeting |
| quail eggs | container |
| bird's nest | plastic dish |
| cowie picks | oasis |

1.

2.

3.

## DESIGN

1. Choose a container with an outdoor wood-
   land feel, such as a piece of mossy pottery or a
   weathered, galvanized pot. Line the container
   with plastic so the water won't soak into the
   pot's surface. Trim the oasis, using whatever
   pieces you need to keep it firmly wedged in
   the container without tape. Begin the design
   by inserting a twig or piece of budded
   forsythia off center, to create your line.

2. Add flowers, incorporating the tallest to the
   smallest. This will enable you to create an
   open, airy arrangement. Leave space for the
   vignettes. Add small buds to add texture to
   the arrangement.

**4.**

3. Now, begin to create seasonal vignettes, such as a bird's nest with eggs or birch bark and mushrooms. If you use birch bark, take it from the forest floor, rather than a living tree. To use bulbs, remove them from the pot, wash the dirt off, and cut off the stem at the base. You can condition the stem by putting it in fresh water for a few minutes before inserting it in the oasis.

4. Add mushrooms to finish.

## color options

THIS ARRANGEMENT FEATURES practically every springtime color and flower. Feel free to experiment, though.

We suggest (top to bottom):

1. white orchid

2. glory lily

3. iceland poppy

4. yellow dahlia

5. jasmine

# Zen Reflection

This centerpiece is meant to stimulate spiritual conversation while, at the same time, letting your imagination run free. Imagine an open space with a stream of water dancing off the aged, polished stones that lie beneath the flowers.

### FLOWERS

sheet moss
2 stems pink spray roses
3–5 chartreuse dendrobium
  orchids
3–5 strands of bear grass

### MATERIALS

10-inch salad plate
water
oasis (igloo-shaped)
river stones
galax leaf
wire
clear silicone
glue gun

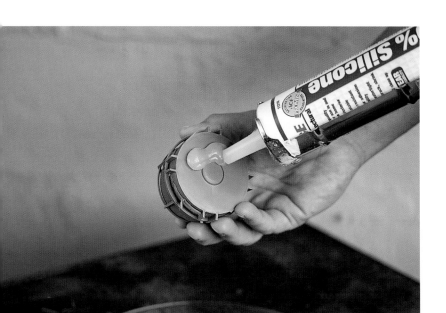

1.

1. Use a glue gun to put glue on the bottom of your igloo oasis. Stick it to your dish and let it dry for a few minutes. The igloo is going to give shape to your arrangement.

2. Spray the moss with water until it is damp. Cover the igloo with the moss. If the moss won't stick, cut the wire you have into small pieces and use those pieces as pins.

3. Poke holes in the center of the moss and igloo with the wire, then insert the orchids into the holes. If the holes aren't big enough, use a pen or pencil to widen them.

2.

3.

4. Take three strands of bear grass, twist them with wire, and insert them in the center of the igloo. Using five galax leaves, arrange them in the igloo at various heights. Insert all the buds and flowers of two stems of hot pink spray roses deep and low in the igloo, with perhaps one or two flowers rising a little higher, but not as tall as the orchids.

5. Add ¼ cup of water to the plate. Add a variety of polished river stones scattered on the plate and resting in the water.

IT'S POSSIBLE TO ADD SOME excitement to this arrangement with the addition of bold color.

We suggest (top to bottom):

1. pink calla lily

2. yellow and red parrot tulip

3. pink ranuncula

4. blue marguerite

5. pink china mum

4.

# CHAPTER 5

## Bridal Bouquets

# Spring Bouquet

We created this bouquet on a whim one year for our annual wedding show and it has been a favorite ever since. It evokes the essence of spring in both fragrance and color. It has clean colors, but the effect is very textured, which makes it an interesting piece for any bride to carry.

*FLOWERS*

18 *white tulips*
20 *purple muscaris*
5 *white lilacs*

*MATERIALS*

*ribbon*

1.

## DESIGN

1. Take your tulips and bunch them together in your hand, then collar the tulips with the lilacs, three quarters of the way around. Finally, take your muscaris and lay them on the white lilac. This creates a tiered look for the bouquet, more crescent-shaped than round.

2. Choose a coordinating ribbon that will complement the periwinkle blue of the muscari.

LILACS, LIKE MANY FLOWERS (ESPECIALLY WHITE ONES) ARE HIGHLY FRAGRANT. BE SURE TO ASK YOUR BRIDE AND HER ATTENDANTS ABOUT ANY SENSITIVITIES THEY MAY HAVE TO CERTAIN FRAGRANCES BEFORE DECIDING ON WHAT FLOWERS TO INCLUDE IN THE BOUQUETS.

**3.**

3. French-braid the stems together, beginning about 3 inches from the bottom of the bouquet and working to the top. Give the stems a fresh cut, in proportion to the length of the ribbon and the height of the person carrying the bouquet.

## color options

BRIDES WHO GET MARRIED IN the spring have so many wonderful flower options. Of course, they will often choose to have their floral colors match the bridal party colors. However, we never hesitate to suggest that they pick glorious spring flowers and have the dresses match those hues!

We suggest (top to bottom):

1. pink/red bougainvillea

2. lily of the valley

3. pink spider lily

4. pink indian hawthorne

5. red hibiscus

# Summer Bouquet

This bouquet perfectly complements a summer bride who has chosen cool colors as her palette. Perhaps her bridesmaids would wear the sherbetlike colors of periwinkle, lavender, cream, yellow, or sage green. Her tablecloths and other dressings would also feature these types of colors.

This bridal bouquet features a mix of whites as well as soft greens. Even choosing one dominant color, such as white, allows you to play with color—there are creams, yellow-whites, and even green-white flowers. And, of course, each type of rose looks a little different from every other. These variations create texture and depth in the arrangement. Finally, the crystals in the stephanotis pick up the light and shimmer.

### FLOWERS

*1 bunch curly parsley*
*10–12 'Bianca' roses (white)*
*9 'Limona' roses (chartreuse)*
*9 'Vendela' roses (cream-colored)*

*18 stephanotis florets*
*1 package Austrian crystal stems*
*1 bunch vibernum greens*

### MATERIALS

*damask ribbon*
*chenille pipe cleaners*
*Austrian crystal stems*
*stephanotis stems*
*green floral tape*

1.                                    3.                                    4–5.

## DESIGN

1. Remove the stephanotis stems from the box
   and soak them in water for five minutes. Insert
   a flower and a crystal into each stem. Place
   them into a dry oasis to keep them standing
   and separate from each other. Keep them moist
   and spray them with water and preservative.
   Bind them in clusters of three or five. Set aside.

2. Gather your flowers at your workstation and
   strip them of foliage from the neck down.
   After you have prepped them, make sure you
   keep each type together, but not in such tight
   bunches that they bruise. They do not need to
   be kept in water.

3. Take a few of the 'Vendela' roses in one hand,
   in a tight bunch. Then add some viburnum,
   making the bouquet round by turning it as
   you add flowers. Lay the stems next to each
   other as you work. Some stems may cross, but
   you don't need to interweave all the stems
   because the bouquet doesn't need to stand on
   its own.

FOR BOUTONNIERES FOR THE
GENTLEMEN IN THE WEDDING
PARTY, USE THE SAME TYPES OF
ROSES AS IN THE BOUQUET.

6.

7.

8.

4. Add the stephanotis clusters to the bouquet.

5. For a background accent, add parsley as you move outward, tucking it in deeper than the flowers. Think of these additions as adding a third dimension to the bouquet.

6. Once you have the bouquet in place, attach the pipe cleaners as high as possible below the neck of the bouquet. Twist a couple of times to get it tight, but be careful not to break the neck of the roses. Either put the flowers in water or lay them over an oasis so the petals don't bruise against your table as you get the ribbon. Choose a ribbon that picks up the color and texture of the bridal gown. Starting with too much ribbon is better than getting too little at first.

7. Place the ribbon so that the two tails are facing you. Pick up one tail and wrap it fully around the bouquet, then make a bow. Cut the ends of the ribbon in a dovetail.

8. Give the bouquet a fresh cut with the clippers, but don't cut your stems as short as you want them until you're ready to deliver the flowers to the bride. Keep them in water until as late as possible. When transporting the bouquet, wrap the bottom in a wet paper towel, and insert that into a plastic bag. Make sure you protect the ribbon from getting wet.

# Fall Bouquet

This bouquet is rich in color and lush in texture. Many brides today are choosing to pick up the color of their attendants' dresses, and for a fall wedding, this will flatter the bridesmaids as well as the setting.

## FLOWERS

4 green viburnums
10 burgundy mini calla lilies
5 chartreuse cymbidium
   orchids with burgundy
   throats
5 burgundy hypericums
8 stems of chartreuse roses

## MATERIALS

cording
stemmed jewels
corsage tape
assistant wires
6 lady's apples
tissue
floral tape

1.                                        2a.                                        2b.

## DESIGN

1. Wire the apples: Hold the apple in your hand with the stem up. At the bottom of the apple, insert one wire horizontally. Then do the same thing, but from the opposite direction. Your wires should end up in an "X." Take two of the wire ends and pull them together, then do the same with the remaining two.

2. Wire the orchids: Take a lightweight wire and a small piece of napkin or tissue. Wet your fingers and roll the piece of tissue onto the middle of the wire. Insert the wire from the top of the flowers into the throat of the orchid, ending up with two lengths on each side of the stem. Take one more length of wire and insert it horizontally, just below the flowers but at the top of the stem. Bring the wire on each side down to the stem of the orchid. Using floral tape, cover the wire and stem together.

3.                          4.                          5.

3. Wire the jewels: First, take the number of stemmed jewels that you want to use off the main stem. Next, use a medium-weight wire and place it vertically next to the stem of the jewel. Using green floral tape, tape the wires together.

4. Clean all foliage from under the blossoms of your flowers. Now, gather all of the flowers together and arrange the bouquet in a circle, balancing the colors and textures in a way that appeals to you. Turn the bouquet frequently in your hand to achieve a balance.

   Insert wired jewels in a scattered fashion throughout the bouquet.

5. Tie the bouquet with a cord in a French-braid design. Cut stems in proportion to the wrap.

AUTUMN BOUQUETS USUALLY feature deep reds and wine colors, but you can also use deep oranges and dark yellows. We suggest (top to bottom):

1. red gerber daisy

2. china mum

3. pink dahlia

4. orange and yellow orchid

5. purple and yellow primrose

6. purple coneflower

# Winter Bouquet

Some brides want a pretty look, while others opt for drama, particularly in winter. This bouquet exudes strength, determination, boldness, and a touch of flamboyance! If the feather boa is a bit much for you, the ribbon is fine on its own.

*FLOWERS*

2-foot long branch of white
    pine, broken into sprigs
18 red roses

*MATERIALS*

7 Austrian crystals
satin ribbon
18-inch feather boa
floral tape

1.

2.

## DESIGN

1. Wire Austrian crystals by taping them.

2. Arrange flowers in your hand in a round
   bouquet, inserting white pine and crystals as
   you go along. Remember to turn the bouquet
   as you are designing. This allows you to see
   the bouquet in its entirety and check for
   fullness.

IF YOU'RE TRANSPORTING
FLOWERS IN TEMPERATURES
BELOW 30°F, COVER THEM
WITH PLASTIC TO ENSURE
THAT THEY DON'T FREEZE.

3.

4.

3. Take the white feather boa and make a collar under the bouquet. Using both ends, tie the boa in a knot and clip the ends close to the knot.

4. Cover stems using double-faced satin ribbon, and finish with a three-button collar using pearl-headed pins.

## color options

RED ROSE BOUQUETS CAN BE duplicated with other lush flowers, although the color and bloom changes will also change the feeling of the bouquet. Pink peonies, for example, are more fun, while white roses are more innocent and less dramatic. However, for a unique look, we suggest (top to bottom):

1. calla lily

2. queen protea

# Bridal Shower Luncheon

Separate tussie mussie bouquets are grouped together, each tied with its own ribbon. As your guests are getting ready to leave, you simply pull one of the bouquets from the arrangement and hand it to them as a token of appreciation. A perfect ending to a perfect luncheon.

## FLOWERS

3 bunches pink spray roses
1 bunch white wax flower
20 white alstromerias
1 bunch pink bouvardia
12 osiana roses
10 stems lavender godetia
1 bunch Italian variegated
   pittisporum

## MATERIALS

silver revere bowl
½ yard of 4-inch French silk
   ribbon
approximately 4 yards
   1½-inch satin ribbon
   (estimate 1 yard per guest)
floral tape
water
knife
scissors
clippers

1.

2.

3.

## DESIGN

1. Add water to your container. It should hold as many individual small bouquets as there are guests. Follow instructions for bouquet turning to make individual bouquets of the small flowers.

2. Wrap floral tape around the neck of each bouquet.

3. Pull one of the wires on the edge of the ribbon to create a ruffle.

4. Add the ruffle to the bouquet as a collar, twisting the wires left over from the ribbon to secure it.

4.

5.

6.

5. Choose a narrow ribbon (we suggest a double-faced satin), approximately one yard in length, and tie the ribbon and knot under the French ribbon ruffle. Be sure to leave long ribbon tails on the narrow ribbon.

6. Give the stems of each tussie mussie bouquet a fresh cut, and then carefully arrange the tussie mussies in the container in a mound shape, leaving long ribbon tails hanging outside the container.

7. Place the arrangement in the center of the table and extend a ribbon to each guest's seat.

## color options

THESE FLOWERS ARE VERY feminine and colorful and look beautiful at the center of any table.

We suggest (top to bottom):

1. mini monumosas

2. red primrose

3. purple cornflower

4. purple Japanese wisteria

5. lavender

6. bromeliads

7. Chinese lantern

# CHAPTER 6

## Seasonal Arrangements

# Romancing Spring

Envision yourself in your garden on a beautifully warm spring day, enjoying nature's glorious response to the sun. We named this arrangement Romancing Spring because peonies are the last flower to say good-bye to spring and hello to summer.

## FLOWERS

5–10 ferns
10 peonies

## MATERIALS

oasis
plastic container
basket with handle
ribbon
clippers
floral tape
cowie picks

1.

2.

3.

1. Line your basket with a plastic liner. Soak the oasis and secure it in the basket liner using ¼-inch tape. Cut the peonies with a knife about 6 inches from the blossom and insert them in one half of the basket. Save the longer stem lengths and set them aside—do not discard. Add greens to the arrangement to cover the oasis. It will look as if the bouquet is resting on a bed of greens.

2. Once the peonies are arranged in place, insert the stems in the oasis opposite the peony heads (on the other side of the basket), thus creating the illusion of a gathering of peonies.

3. Make a bow and place it on a pick. Insert ribbon between the flowers' stems and heads, covering any other part of the oasis.

4. Dovetail ribbon ends for a finished look.

TO REVIVE DROOPY FLOWERS,

TRIM THEIR STEMS A BIT AND

LAY THEM HORIZONTALLY IN

WARM WATER.

It's beach party time! This arrangement is a gem for the oceanside clambake or elegant beachfront party. Your partygoers can enjoy the rewards of your frolics and jaunts through the waves and sand to collect the seashells used in this arrangement. It's festive, it's funky, and it's simple!

### FLOWERS

*5–6 pink gerberas*
*bear grass*

### MATERIALS

*2-inch satin ribbon*
*1½-inch ribbon*
*shells*
*glass cylinder*
*oasis*
*plastic liner*
*clippers*
*knife*
*double-sided tape*
*sheet moss*

**1.**

### DESIGN

1. Fill your cylinder with seashells, using a variety of shapes and sizes. Put your oasis in a plastic liner that fits the opening of the cylinder. Although there will be space in the cylinder around the shells, make sure they are packed tightly enough to stay in place. Cover the oasis with a damp sheet moss.

2.

3.

2. Place the gerberas and the bear grass in the moss, using a pencil if necessary to make holes for the stems.

3. Use double-sided tape to secure a ribbon that will cover the oasis and liner at the top of the cylinder.

4. Wrap a second ribbon around the first. It's your choice to tie a bow or knot at this point, depending on whether you want a formal or casual look. You can use double-sided tape to secure the first ribbon before tying a knot with the second ribbon.

4.

# Fall Whispers

This centerpiece presentation is very evocative—you can almost hear the rustling of the leaves on a fall day. Yet it exudes rich warmth in its setting, lending itself to the perfect whisper of a fall dinner party.

| FLOWERS | MATERIALS |
|---|---|
| 15 'Leonides' roses | pipe cleaner |
| rose petals | ribbon |
| leaves | clippers |
| | knife |

1.

## DESIGN

1. Strip all leaves and guard petals from the roses.

2. Using your hand, create a round bouquet, once again remembering to turn the bouquet to ensure fullness and a round shape.

3. Using a chenille or pipe cleaner, tie the bouquet, twisting securely but not so tightly as to damage the stems or flowers.

2.

THE MORE FOLIAGE YOU REMOVE FROM THE STEM OF A FLOWER, THE MORE NUTRIENTS WILL GO TO THE BLOSSOM. HOWEVER, YOU MAY NOT WANT TO REMOVE ALL OF THE LEAVES, AS THAT CAN LOOK UNNATURAL.

3.

4.

5.

4. Tie the bouquet with your ribbon, making a soft bow tucked up under the neck of the bouquet.

5. Using clippers, cut stems evenly across the bottom.

6. Gently, but firmly, give the bouquet stems a tap on the table. Create the illusion that the centerpiece is sitting in a bed of rose petals and fallen autumn leaves by arranging the petals and leaves on the tablecloth close to the bouquet, tucking some in between the stems. This centerpiece generally lasts for five hours with no water source.

## color options

TO REMAIN TRUE TO THE SPIRIT of autumn, it's important to use flowers that have deep colors, but if you'd like to use this arrangement with a softer palette, pinks and whites would work well.

We suggest (top to bottom):

1. pink dahlia

2. jasmine

# Winter Lights

Dazzle your friends with this spectacular two-tiered creation.
This all-white arrangement, with a hint of sparkle, lights up
any room, especially if there is snow outside the windows.

## FLOWERS

20 white tulips
3 gardenias
2 icicle branches

## MATERIALS

ribbon
white stones
3 2-inch floating candles
vase
water
knife
pedestal dish
low-floating bowl
pearl-headed corsage pins
floral tape

2.

3.

4.

*DESIGN*

1. Take two bunches of white field tulips in your hand and arrange into a round bouquet.

2. To secure these tulips in their desired form, wrap a 2-inch-wide length of floral tape around the stems.

3. Next, cover the tape with a band of 2-inch-wide ribbon (we chose ribbon that has sparkles on it). Now, folding over one end, secure with two or three pearl-headed pins.

4. Cut stems straight across and even with a knife (not clippers) by laying them gently on the table.

5. Take the arrangement of tulips and tap the bottom of the stems on the table.

6. Stand the tulips in the candy dish and add white stones around the stems. You might need to use pins to secure the tulips in an upright fashion.

7. As a base, use a low glass bowl (floating lotus bowl). Next, take a clear glass pedestal dish (i.e., a candy dish). To begin the process, place the candy dish inside the glass bowl. Add water to the candy dish and the lower bowl. Add three floating candles and the three gardenias to the lower bowl. Light the candles at the appropriate hour, allowing a burning time of three to five hours.

6.

7.

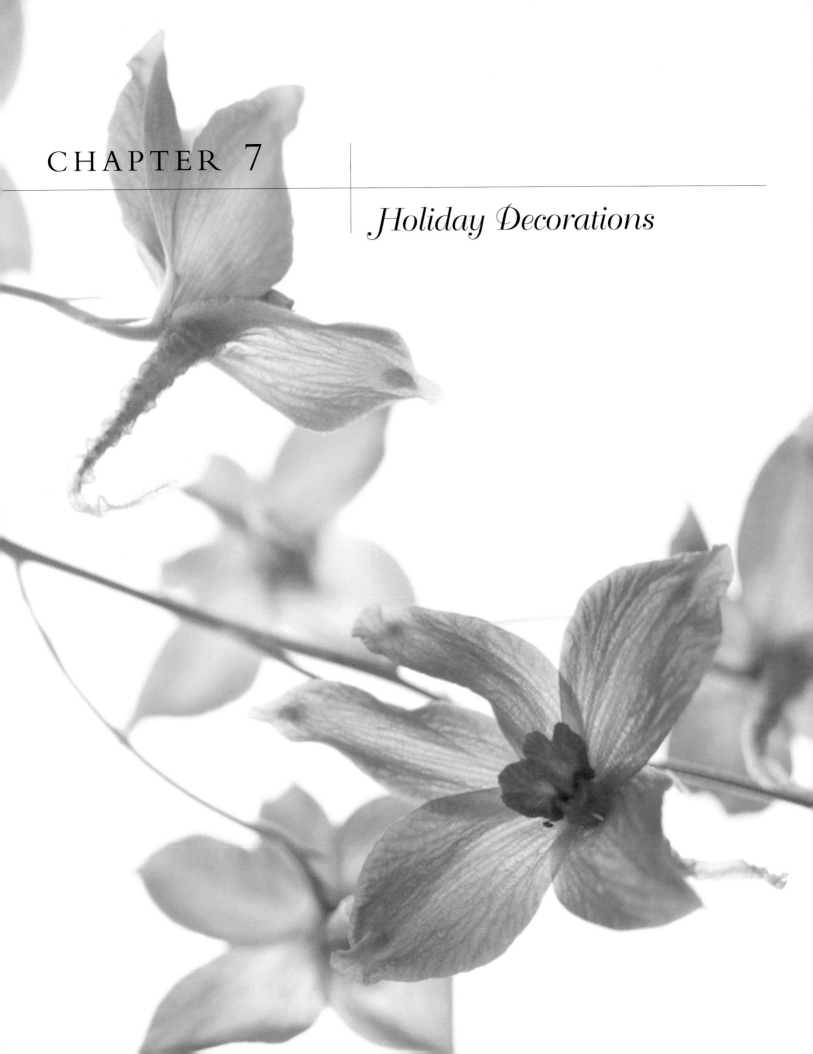

# CHAPTER 7

*Holiday Decorations*

# Autumn Pleasure

This centerpiece uses natural elements of the season to put the finishing touches on your holiday table. This design is a little challenging, so you'll feel a real sense of accomplishment when it's complete.

## FLOWERS

5 grevilleas
8 crespedias
7 mango mini calla lilies
9 chartreuse viking poms
5–10 seeded eucalyptus
9 hypericums
10 alstromerias
½ bunch leather leaf
a few strands of bittersweet
3 Asiatic lilies

## MATERIALS

grapevine
3 oases (igloo-shaped)
moss
pinecones
10 lady's apples
chenille
cowie picks

clippers
knife
votive
croton leaf
raffia
rubber band

1–2.

3.

## DESIGN

1. Cut a length of grapevine and mold it into the shape of an elongated figure eight, using green chenille to secure it. Place the grapevine in the center of the table.

2. Take three oasis igloos, soaked in water, and place them strategically along the grapevine. Arrange greens and leaves in the igloos along the grapevine form. Be sure to follow the lines of the shape when setting in the greens.

3. Place the flowers along the grapevine, creating an arrangement rich in texture and color.

 PRIOR TO YOUR DINNER, PLACE THE VOTIVES IN THE FRIDGE—THEY'LL BURN SLOWER.

4.

5.

4. Tuck fall leaves into the arrangement.

5. Intersperse pinecones, lady's apples, and hypericum berries throughout the arrangement. To warm up the piece and set the holiday mood, add candlelight by taking croton leaves, wrapping them around a votive glass, and securing them in place with an elastic band. Then tie the leaf on with raffia, overlaying the rubber band so it is not seen.

color options

IT'S POSSIBLE TO CHANGE THIS arrangement not just with different flowers, but also with other greens.

We suggest (top to bottom):

 1. orange gerber daisy

 2. orange marigold

 3. pink ranuncula

 4. orange Iceland poppy

 5. thistle

# Bread and Onion

Although this arrangement contains both a vegetable and a flower, they actually belong to the same family! The bullet allium is from the onion family, so it's not really a marriage of opposites at all.

## FLOWERS

3–4 anemones
5–7 orange poppies
7 bullet alliums

## MATERIALS

seeded eucalyptus
round loaf of bread
9 white onions
oasis
plastic container
cowie picks
clippers
floral knife

1-2.

3.

*DESIGN*

1. Use a large, round Tuscan loaf of bread. We recommend ordering a 16-inch round—it seems to work best. Slice off the top (only about an inch) and set it aside.

2. Scoop out the inside of the bread. Insert a plastic liner that fits within the opening, keeping the rim an inch below the bread, then add oasis to the liner.

3. Take your onions (choosing by size in proportion to the loaf of bread), remove outer skins, and place the onions into the oasis with 6-inch cowie picks so that the oasis is covered.

4-5.

4. Arrange the allium stems among the onions toward the center of the bread, at varying heights.

5. Add the poppies and anemones. Begin with the larger flowers and fill in with more allium.

6. Add seeded eucalyptus, and the outer skins from the onions to cover up any gaps through which you can see the oasis.

6.

## color options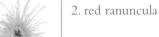

THIS ARRANGEMENT NOW features a blue and orange focus, but it could easily work with yellow and red.

We suggest (top to bottom):

1. red anthurium

2. red ranuncula

3. yellow spider mum

# Majestic Topiary &
# Resplendent Staircase

Decorate your staircase in a scintillating manner for the holidays. Create a focal piece in your home for all who enter with this distinguished topiary and regal garland. Make it elegant, make it radiant, make it out-of-this-world!

## MAJESTIC TOPIARY

3-foot tall, 1½-inch sapling
  (you can use any type
  of tree that you like)
1 bunch cedar greens
1 bunch white pine greens
1 bunch balsam greens
1 bunch boxwood greens

8-inch oasis sphere
chicken wire
clippers
wire cutters
cowie picks
5–10 plumber's helpers
sapling covering
sleeve ribbon

## RESPLENDENT STAIRCASE

7 yards garland (real or silk)
7 bunches of hydrangea
  (real or silk)

7 yards rich fabric
  (45 inches wide)
chenille stems
water tubes
  (if using real hydrangea)

1.

2.

3.

## MAJESTIC TOPIARY DESIGN

1. Cage the 8-inch oasis sphere using 1-inch diameter chicken wire and place it in water to soak for approximately one hour, allowing for full absorption.

2. Place the caged oasis sphere on the sapling, inserting the sapling through the center of the sphere until the wire hooks onto the sapling.

3. Add greens, which will be held by the cage that also keeps the oasis in place.

4. Make three ribbon bows.

5. Insert one bow in the middle of the greened sphere, equidistant between the top and bottom of the topiary, then place the other two bows equidistant from one another around the sphere.

6. Cut three lengths of the same ribbon to loop from bow to bow around the topiary, giving the illusion that they are connected to one another. Wire the ribbon to 6-inch cowie picks and insert in the topiary.

5.

6.

TOPIARIES ARE GREEN, OF
course, and few color options
exist. However, you can use
different background greens to
change the texture of this
arrangement.

We suggest:

1. lemon leaf

2. leather leaf

3. pittosporum

1.

2.

3.

STAIRCASE DECORATIONS ARE
ONE OF THE SIMPLEST THINGS
YOU CAN DO TO WELCOME
THE HOLIDAYS INTO YOUR
HOME. EVEN IF YOU CHOOSE
TO USE ARTIFICIAL GREENS
EACH HOLIDAY SEASON, WE
RECOMMEND CHANGING THE
RIBBONS EVERY YEAR TO
KEEP THE APPEARANCE FRESH
AND SURPRISING.

## RESPLENDENT STAIRCASE DESIGN

1. Purchase garland roping from your local nursery and swag the garland in equal drapes along your staircase.

2. Next take your fabric and lay it over the garland, without fully covering it, but instead using it as an accent to the material.

3. Place topiary trees at various intervals along the staircase. Secure the trees with chenille stems by attaching to a railing or newel post on the staircase.

4.

5.

4. Put hydrangea stems in water tubes.

5. Place the hydrangea near topiary trees at the banisters.

## color options

YOUR RIBBONS AND FLOWERS should complement the greens, as well as the decor of your home. And, of course, they should carry the theme of your holiday celebration.

We suggest (top to bottom):

1. pink bougainvillea

2. white gardenia

# A Touch of Whimsy

And he came to life one day! The child in all of us comes alive when we see this project. (And it's not a bad project to do with a child, for that matter.) Even the snowman is delighted; sometimes it seems as if he's about to dance off the table.

FLOWERS

6–7 dozen white mums
2 icicle branches
carrot
raspberries

MATERIALS

8-inch, 6-inch, and
  4-inch oasis spheres
ribbon
hat
8-inch clear saucer
sparkles
spray adhesive
clippers
knife
dowel

2–3.

4.

5.

## DESIGN

1. Take the three spheres of oasis and soak for approximately one hour.

2. Take the 8-inch ball and slice off a sliver of oasis to create stability. Place in an 8-inch, clear, round saucer and insert the ¼-inch wooden dowel in the center of the 8-inch ball.

3. Cutting flowers from stems to 2 inches in length, begin inserting them in the oasis.

4. Take the 6-inch sphere and insert it over the dowel so that it comes to rest on the 8-inch sphere. Add flowers.

5. Take the 4-inch sphere, repeating above steps and covering it with the remaining flowers.

6.

7.

8.

6. Insert blossoms covering the oasis to complete the snowman, using the largest blossoms on the bottom sphere, until completely covered. Clip the dowel to 2 inches above the top of the flowers.

7. Decorate the snowman with a traditional scarf by taking a one-yard length of ribbon and looping it around the neck of the snowman in a simple knot. Cut the ends of the ribbon in dovetail fashion for a completed look. Using ice-covered twig arms and creative resources for hat, eyes, and vest buttons, decorate this magical man.

For the nose, take a baby carrot, clip a 24-gauge wire to 2 inches, insert the carrot in the nonpointed end, and stick the wire in the oasis.

8. Lay out newspapers under the snowman to prepare and protect the surface for the spray glue and glitter. Using the spray glue, lightly coat the snowman and sprinkle him with glitter to resemble snow.

# Magnificent Mantle

This piece lends itself to a formal, sophisticated atmosphere, resting on the mantle in understated elegance. The blending of luxurious red roses and tulips with white genestra is a splendid creative look.

## FLOWERS

3 stems white branches
20 red field tulips
1 bunch white genestra
24 red roses
3–5 seeded eucalyptus
1 bunch spruce
1 bunch cedar
1 bunch white pine
1 bunch boxwood
2 bunches blue juniper berries

## MATERIALS

oasis
window box tray
gold glitter
waterproof tape
cowie sticks
clippers
ribbon

2.

3.

## DESIGN

1. Using a window box tray that fits the measurements of the mantle, prepare it with oasis and ¼-inch green waterproof tape.

2. Using winter greens such as incense cedar, boxwood, white pine, and balsam, green the entire mantle to the desired length, scaling back to front with taller to shorter lengths of greens.

3. Add crystal or white branches throughout the entire arrangement. Place flowers in the same manner as the greens, creating a nice blend of texture using the variety of flowers. Add genestra.

4.

4. Weave 2-inch-wide ribbon throughout the length of the arrangement. Spray very lightly with gold glitter.

5. Place on the mantle.

## color options

THESE EXOTIC FLOWERS LEND A sophisticated air to mantles during the rest of the year.

We suggest (top to bottom):

1. stargazer lily

2. red anthurium

3. white orchid

4. pink china mum

5. red kalanchoe

6. red amarylis

# Tulips in the Snow

We specifically designed this for the Christmas season. We thought it would let everyone feel as if spring was almost here, since tulips burst through the last signs of Old Man Winter.

### FLOWERS
30–40 parrot tulips

### MATERIALS
a few handfuls polyester
  batting
a handful silver glitter
clippers
floral knife
oasis
silver urn
spray adhesive
clear waterproof tape or
  floral tape

2.

3.

## DESIGN

1. Line urn if necessary for protection.

2. Insert tulips in the manner of a growing garden, but keep in mind the arrangement's placement. If this will be a centerpiece, create a rounded arrangement that can be viewed from all sides. If it will be placed where it is viewed from only one angle, insert tulips with more drama in the front.

3. Add polyester batting for snow in clumps to cover the oasis.

4. Spray the tulips and the batting used for snow with glue. Shake silver glitter gently over the arrangement to give the feel of snow.

4.

# CHAPTER 8

*Luncheons*

# By the Beautiful Sea

What lies beneath the sea in uncharted waters comes alive on
your dinner table. This unique combination of "surf & turf"
delights everyone. The accents of sand and small seashells give
an added sense of place.

### FLOWERS

3 yellow freesias
5 strands of bear grass
3 blue delphiniums
2 stems orange spray roses

### MATERIALS

conch with oasis
shells
sand
moss
clippers

**2.**

THIS ARRANGEMENT, AND OTHERS LIKE IT, CAN BE ADAPTED FOR ALL SEASONS. JUST CONSIDER WHAT NATURAL ELEMENTS ARE ABUNDANT DURING A SPECIFIC TIME OF THE YEAR (ACORNS AND LEAVES FOR AUTUMN, PINECONES AND FIR FOR WINTER), AND USE THOSE ELEMENTS TO ACCESSORIZE ANY SEASONAL BLOOMS. ALSO, NOTE THAT YOU DON'T HAVE TO RELY ON SCAVENGING THE BEACH OR FOREST FOR YOUR OUTDOOR ACCESSORIES. MANY CRAFT SHOPS SELL PREPACKAGED SHELLS AND OTHER TRIMMINGS.

## DESIGN

1. Fill the conch shell with wet oasis, cut into a wedge. Packed tightly, it will not need to be taped.

2. Arrange your flowers in a wispy, open, and airy manner. Place the taller ones in first, again setting your lines. Add smaller ones, some in deep to create depth in the arrangement.

3.

4.

3. Add a few strands of bear grass bursting from the shell to give the illusion of dune grass. Add moss to cover your oasis.

4. Sprinkle sand on the table and place the conch in the center. Place some small shells around it.

## color options

CHOOSE FLOWERS THAT LOOK appropriate next to sand and shell tones, such as pale pinks and oranges. White is also a common color for beach flowers.

We suggest (top to bottom):

1. pink coneflower

2. orange orchid

3. white gardenia

# Gilding the Lily

This design is proper, formal, and regal. We always think of it as "The Lady."

### FLOWERS
*sheet moss*
*7 pink Asiatic lilies*

### MATERIALS
*pot with oasis*
*ribbon*
*scissors*
*clippers*
*wire (optional)*

2.

3.

4.

Ce WHEN WORKING WITH LILIES,
ALWAYS CLEAN THE STAMENS.
AS THE LILY MATURES, THE
STAMEN BECOMES LESS
SUBSTANTIAL AND MORE
POWDERY, WHICH CAN MAKE
THE ARRANGEMENT DUSTY.
IF THE POWDER BEGINS TO
SHOW, USE A PIPE CLEANER TO
BRUSH THE LILY PETALS. AND,
BY THE WAY, A PIPE CLEANER
WILL ALSO TAKE THE LILY
POWDER OFF YOUR CLOTHES.
DON'T USE WATER; IT MAKES
THE POWDER STICK.

### DESIGN

1. Place the oasis in your container. In this arrangement there is no need to tape it down. Remove all leaves from the stems of the lilies.

2. Leaving stems long, create a bouquet. Because longer stems are harder to manipulate, this will take more time than the creation of your other bouquets.

3. Cut stems to length, using the container they will be set in as a guide.

5.  6.  7.

4. Check the stems to be sure they are in proportion to the size of the container.

5. Insert into the middle of the oasis at a proportional height.

6. Take two lengths of ribbon and tie the ribbon under the neck of the lilies into two bows, one on each side.

7. Cover the oasis completely with moss.

LILIES REALLY DO WORK BEST for this arrangement, however, within the lily family there are many color options.

We suggest (top to bottom):

1. stargazer lily

2. orange tiger lily

# Pots of Sunshine

Always turn your face toward the sunshine and the shadows
will fall behind you. This arrangement, glorious in color, will
radiate from your table. Purple and yellow are a splendid
combination. Although this is a simple creation, it leaves a
lasting impression.

### FLOWERS

5–8 sunflowers
half bunch of purple statice

### MATERIALS

terra-cotta pots
votives
aluminum foil
oasis
ribbon
glue gun

1.

2.

SHORT SUNFLOWERS ARE
RARELY FOUND IN GARDENS
BECAUSE SO MANY PEOPLE
LOVE THEIR HEIGHT AS MUCH
AS THEIR WIDE FACES. BUT
THEY ARE WIDELY AVAILABLE
AT FLORAL SHOPS.

## DESIGN

1. Line a terra-cotta pot with plastic and fill with wet oasis. Insert your sunflowers at a slight angle around the rim of the pot and then insert the remaining 1–3 stems in the middle.

2. Ring the rim of the pot with purple statice and position it here and there among the other flowers toward the center.

3.

4.

3. Using miniature terra-cotta pots, make shells of aluminum foil and insert them in pots for votive candles.

4. Decorate the miniature terra-cotta pots with ribbon and a touch of statice as accents, and place them around the larger pot. Use a glue gun to attach the pieces of statice to the ribbon.

## color options

MANY FLOWERS HAVE A HAPPY, sunflower type of appeal, which is the effect you want to create with this arrangement.

We suggest (top to bottom):

1. pink gerberas

2. purple thistle

# Strawberry Festivals

Have your own annual strawberry festival. A daisy bouquet with a collar of strawberries will make your summertime guests' mouths water. Quick, somebody grab the whipped cream!

FLOWERS

20 daisies
2 large handfuls moss
2 quarts strawberries

MATERIALS

basket
cowie picks
clippers
floral knife
plastic oasis
waterproof tape

**1.**

**2.**

**3.**

1. Arrange daisies to look like a growing garden. The flowers should be at varying heights.

2. Arrange moss at the base of the flower stems to hide the oasis. The moss can be somewhat clumpy to give a more natural appearance.

3. Insert cowie picks through strawberries and secure to the border of your arrangement.

STRAWBERRIES ARE A DELICATE FOOD AND THIS ARRANGEMENT IS ONLY GOOD FOR ONE DAY. IF YOU WANT TO DO AN ARRANGEMENT LIKE THIS BUT NEED IT TO LAST LONGER, MANY CRAFT STORES AND FLORAL SUPPLIERS HAVE BEADED AND CLOTH STRAWBERRIES, WHICH CAN ALSO ADD SOME WHIMSY TO THE TABLE.

Perfect for last-minute plans to entertain the unexpected guest, this arrangement is simple, yet elegant in a casual sort of way. You can dress it up by adding some unique characteristics, as we did here.

*FLOWERS*

*12 blue irises*
*3–5 stems Italian variegated*
   *pittosporum*

*MATERIALS*

*gift bag or luminary*
*1½ yards of 2-inch ribbon*
*oasis*
*scissors*
*clippers*
*knife*
*plastic container*

1.

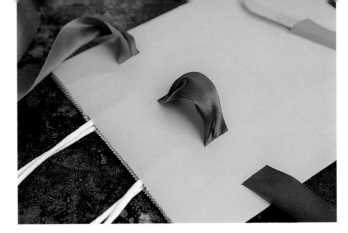

2a.

2b.

3.

## DESIGN

1. Cut two vertical slits in the front and back of each bag, three fourths of the way up, as well as one on each of the sides.

2. Weave ribbon through slits, leaving enough ribbon on each end to tie a bow.

3. Insert a plastic container with oasis in each bag so that it fits snugly. Arrange irises in a free-form manner.

4. Fill in any gaps with a few greens, keeping them lower than the iris and just peeking out from the top of the bag.

YOU CAN ACHIEVE A VARIETY OF LOOKS FOR THIS ARRANGEMENT BY USING DIFFERENT TOOLS TO MAKE THE HOLES IN YOUR BAGS, SUCH AS A HOLE PUNCH OR SHEARING SCISSORS.

# RESOURCES

We invite you to go to www.danamarkos.com for more information about these arrangements, as well as our other services and ideas.

Most local florists can order any type of flower, assuming it's in season, and can also help you get any materials for making arrangements.

**SOUTHERN CALIFORNIA:**

Blossom Valley
754 Wall St.
Los Angeles, CA 90014
(213) 891-9320

Stats Floral Supply
34081 Doheny Park Rd.
Capistrano Beach, CA 92624
(949) 493-3752

**NORTHERN CALIFORNIA:**

Florin Center Florist
5961 A Florin Rd.
Sacramento, CA 95823
(916) 422-1410

Yamada's Kiku Floral II
805 E Olive Ave.
Fresno, CA 93728
(559) 264-4540

**PACIFIC NORTHWEST:**

Blooms on Broadway
433 Broadway E.
Seattle, WA 98102
(206) 324-8845

Floral Supply Syndicate
963 Mercer St.
Seattle, WA 98109
(206) 343-1690

**CHICAGO:**

Highland Park Florist
461 Central Ave.
Highland Park, IL 60035
(847) 266 7300

Floral Impressions
2324 N. Cicero Ave.
Chicago, IL 60639
(773) 637-2299

**NEW YORK:**

Embassy Florist
2458 Broadway
New York, NY 10024
(212) 724-8604

Calla Lily Floral & Bridal
39 Hambletonian Rd.
Sugar Loaf, NY 10981
(845) 469-7868

**TEXAS:**

Giovanny's Floral
10848 Westheimer Rd.
Houston, TX 77042
(866) 264-2026

Floral Trends
5301 S. Shaver St.
Houston, TX 77034
(713) 944-3831

**FLORIDA:**

Carnival Flowers & Gifts
9552 S.W. 137th Avenue
Miami, FL 33186
(305) 380-1799

Creative Clutter
1695 W. Indiantown Rd. #16
Jupiter, FL 33458
(866) 746-1005
(www.creativeclutter.cc)

**WASHINGTON, D.C.**

Just for You Flowers
1209 Tuckerman St.
Washington, DC 20011
(202) 882-3418

Abigail's Floral Accessories
Lanham, MD 20706
(301) 577-2022

**BOSTON:**

Boston Blossoms
468 Commonwealth Ave.
Boston, MA 02215
(617) 536-8600

Jacobson Floral Supply Co.
500 Albany St.
Boston, MA 02118
(617) 426-4200

PHOTOGRAPHY CREDITS

All photography by Bobbie Bush Photography, with the exception of:

Photography by Jennifer K. Beal: ii, viii, 4, 12, 14, 17, 23, 134-136

Photography by Burke/Triolo Productions/Picturequest: 1, 6-7, 11, 31 (lower right), 41 (lower right), 45 (right), 51 (lower right), 59 (lower right), 63 (lower right), 67 (lower right), 79 (lower right), 83 (lower right), 89 (lower right), 93 (lower right), 99 (lower right), 107 (lower right), 117 (lower right), 121 (lower right), 125 (lower right)

Photography by Tim Kreiger/Artville: vii, 11 ("green"), 13, 26, 46, 68, 84, 112,

Photography by Peter Margonelli: 4

## ACKNOWLEDGMENTS

I would like to acknowledge and thank my wife Elizabeth, son Daniel, and daughter Amanda for their unending love and support in my passion for flowers and design.
—DANA

I would like to thank my husband Desi and children Kate, Susanne, Michelle, and Monica and my grandchildren for all their love, support, and inspiration through my journey.
—SUSANNE

Together, we would like to thank our staff for their incredible talent and our many friends, extended family, and business associates for their constant support and encouragement.